I'll Try to
Be Short ...

Small Doses of Healthy Humor

*To: Dr. Dobbs,
Many blessings!
Luther Beauchamp
11-22-99*

Luther Beauchamp
Illustrated by Joe McKeever

Kidiot Productions

Published by

Kidiot Productions
P.O. Box 10
Chiefland, Florida 32644
(352) 493-2525

Dedication

Dedicated to the memory of my mother,
Macey Callaway Beauchamp
who died June 22, 1997
and in honor of my father,
W. O. Beauchamp, Sr.

Contents

ForeWARNING!

Some books have a foreword, but in this case, I thought a forewarning might be more appropriate. While it is true that our family has a history of humor, my dad seems to have taken it to the next level. Sometimes, Mom and I wish he were just more level-headed. He has become quite associated with jokes. I remember when I was very young, I often looked at Mom after he told another joke and I pointed to my head, made a circular motion with my hand, and said, "Mom, he's doing it again!"

Despite having to be the guinea pig for most of his jokes, I really am blessed to have a father like him. He has always taken time to spend with me. We began playing one-on-one basketball when we were both small. He used to play on his knees...now I do.

I decided to not only try to justify why my dad continues telling stories, but to warn the reader. If you decide to read this book, you are only encouraging him more. That means that he will tell more and more stories and may even write another book! I am not responsible for what the laughter-inducing material may do. And with that, I will let you make your decision to turn the page or not.

Lance T. Beauchamp

Preface

Trying to be short shouldn't be a problem for a man of my height. For years I have heard the cute comments:

"Stand up, Luther. Oh, you are standing."

"I would ask Luther to stand up...but it wouldn't make that much difference."

"When I came in to the banquet tonight, Luther walked under the table and shook my hand."

My signature opening line as a speaker is "I'll try to be short...How am I doing so far?"

As could be expected of a lawyer I have the tendency to be long-winded in my conversations. When my wife, Vera, complains about it taking me so long to get to the car after church I explain "It's not my fault. Those people wouldn't quit listening!"

She has helped me tremendously to cut out some of the lawyer style and the *repetitiously redundant* language.

A Young Raconteur

We know the man Job of the Old Testament spoke at a very early age. The Bible says, "Job cursed the day he was born."

How early I began entertaining with stories is uncertain, but I do recall my first recorded presentation. When I was in first grade the principal came around to each class with a new-fangled machine I later learned was a reel to reel tape recorder. My teacher suggested I tell my story about the three rabbits.

"Foot died and Foot-Foot got sick. Foot-Foot-Foot called for the doctor, pleading that he not let Foot-Foot die because he already had one Foot in the grave."

Guess What!

Ice cream churns and other luxury items were not easy to acquire during World War II. My parents had placed their order for one from Montgomery Ward in 1943 and the whole family eagerly awaited the arrival.

My four-year-old sister, Frances, was visiting a friend a few blocks away on June 11, 1943 when the friend's mother returned.

"Guess what's new at your house, Frances!"

She jumped with glee and exclaimed, "An ice cream churn!"

Imagine the disappointment that little girl felt when she found out she was wrong. The "new thing" was a baby brother to be named, Robert Luther Beauchamp.

Among the five children (including my brother, three sisters, and myself), Frances is the quietest, least expressive. Some think she never got over the ice cream churn disappointment.

Name That Kid!

My older brother W. O., was named for Daddy who then became Woodrow Ottis Beauchamp, Sr.

I never did learn whether my paternal grandfather, James Riley Beauchamp, put in a bid to have me named for him. But I was named for Mama's daddy, Luther Callaway. For being named Luther, he bought a $25 U. S. Savings Bond for me. (A bribe like that today, probably would be worth about $500.) I don't know how much Grandpa would have had to spend to get them to also give me his middle name, Lafayette.

A Close Call and Deep Roots

During the early years of my law practice, I really wanted the opportunity to serve in the Florida legislature. At 29, I entered a race for state representative in a geographically large district covering several counties in North Florida.

In a very small town I entered the barber shop and requested the votes of the barber and the customer. The barber informed me, "We don't know much about you around here but most of us are country folks."

"I'm sorry about that because I'm a city slicker myself. You see, I was born right downtown in Chiefland." After a brief pause I added, "But my hog pen was only two blocks from city hall."

"I guess that ain't too bad," he acknowledged.

I came dangerously close to being elected!

My statements about place of birth and the location of my livestock project were true. My law office is located within two blocks of my place of birth, two blocks of city hall and in the next block from the former site of my hog pen. My roots are very deep even if there is not much of me above ground.

Doctor's Orders

Grandpa Callaway came up to our house to ask Mama for a piece of fine twine or strong thread about a foot and a half long. Mama told him she would try to find something and inquired as to the intended use.

"Dr. Young gave me these tablets and told me to take one tablet three times each day. If I don't tie a string around it, I won't be able to take it but once."

More Orders

On another visit he said he was on his way to Long Pond, a rather large lake on the south end of Chiefland. When asked why he was going to Long Pond, he explained, "I'm going to wade out into the pond because Dr. Young gave me some medicine and told me to be sure to take it in water."

Weather Wisdom

When it rained, Grandpa would always go for a walk. Even in heavy downpours, he was known to refuse a friend's offer to ride.

On a very cold day, he would say "I like cold weather, but this pleases me too well."

Cozy Cats

When Grandpa saw a romantic couple, he would comment, "She's sticking to him like a sick kitten to a warm brick."

When Postal Service Was Not An Oxymoron

Serving as postmaster for about 30 years, Grandpa Callaway had a lot of memorable experiences. A lady hurriedly entered the post office one day and asked, "Mr. Callaway, what time is the three o'clock mail due?"

Without cracking a smile, he said, "About two-sixty."

She thanked him and left.

He told another customer, who had complained about the price of stamps, that he had a special sale that day. "I can sell you 13 two-cent stamps for a cent and a quarter."

Season's Greetings

As postmaster, Grandpa always gained weight around Christmas time "licking all the syrup off the stamps." He handled many Christmas cards at work and received a lot of them himself.

One comment I remember from him was, "Sometimes I would just as soon get a $5 bill as a Christmas card."

Business Hand

Describing his own handwriting as "a business hand," Grandpa explained that you would have to lay aside all your other business to read it.

Kitten Kasserole

My cousin Riley was about six years old when he was admiring Uncle Sam's litter of baby kittens. The kittens were still nursing at the time and Uncle Sam told Riley, "As soon as they get big enough to eat, I'll give you one of 'em."

With a slow, serious voice Riley responded, "Uncle Sam, we don't eat our kittens."

Favorite Grandchild

When asked which of us five children was his favorite, Grandpa said, "I love one of you just as much as the other, if not better."

Money Matters

Luther Callaway and his brother, Charley, must have resembled each other a lot as teenagers. Grandpa said they looked so much alike that when they went to buy a drink, he would put his hand in Charley's pocket to get the money.

Often he would say he had forgotten to bring any money with him...or leave any anywhere else.

When he got a check cashed or got change back from a purchase, he would count the money and say, "It's all here, but it just is."

Eyes and Ears

Grandpa Callaway told me about two fellows sitting in front of a store building. One asked the other, "Can you see the ant crawling up the utility pole across the street?"

"No, but I can hear his feet slipping."

That Old Big 'Un!

BB guns like fire and money can be used for good or evil.

When I was about 9, I was in the yard with my Red Ryder B-B gun shooting at trees and cans when some older boys across the back fence challenged me to war. Soon after declining their suggestion I felt the sting of a BB on my wrist. Running into the house, crying more from fear than pain I reported it to my oldest sister, Ovieda. She comforted me and told me to stay inside.

A few minutes later, my next oldest sister, Frances and my brother came quickly into the house complaining that when W.O. bent over to pick up a ball he was hit in the seat of the pants with a BB.

Angrily, Ovieda (who had already reached her maximum height of four feet eleven and one-half inches) grabbed my air rifle. With the courage of Teddy Roosevelt and his Rough Riders, she charged into the backyard, cocking and firing the gun as she ran toward the back fence. The 3 boys scrambled for cover as her shots hit the back of their house and BBs pinged against the wringer washing machine on the back porch.

A few days later someone reported that the perpetrators had complained to friends, "We were just trying to have some fun until that old big 'un came out there."

What Goes There?

A Chiefland businessman had store buildings destroyed by fire at two locations within a couple of years. Construction was underway to rebuild on the site of the most recent fire.

My cousin Jamie asked my dad, "Uncle Ottis, what's he going to put in that building?"

Without cracking a smile Daddy responded , "A fire I reckon."

Daddy always believed many fires were caused by insurance policies.

A Paralyzed Stare?

My wife's sister lives in Valdosta, Georgia. Her two sons, Mike and Jeff were elementary school age when they were playing with other children a few houses away.

Mike came running to tell his mother of a near tragedy. "Mama," he said with fear and excitement in his voice, "we were playing in Billy's yard when his mama came home. She didn't see Billy's little brother playing in the driveway until she had almost run over him with the car. When she saw him she slammed on brakes and just sat there *'starelyzed'*!"

How Many Children?

When the Kenny Rogers song, "Lucille" was popular, my nephew Mike was heard singing, "You picked a fine time to leave me, Lucille." Then instead of "four hungry children and a crop in the field..." Mike sang "four *hundred* children..."

Fragile!

When Daddy was serving as a rural mail carrier, one patron had a package in her mail box for him to pick up. On this package, the word, "FRAGILE," did not appear, but these words did: "THIS IS A CLOCK, NOT A BASEBALL."

A Real Bargain

Uncle Willie was on the *conservative side* of the conservative side. He watched his dollars... and his coins.

Discounts were given to him and other family members at Daddy's hardware store. The wife of Daddy's partner in the store, was approached by Uncle Willie with a small box of wood screws with the price of ten cents marked on the box.

"Margie, what's <u>my</u> price on that?"

"Just put the box in your pocket and don't worry about it."

He did!

T.V. or Not T.V.

My youngest sister, Susan came into the house one day and asked "Who left the television off?"

One evening when she was four, Daddy told her to turn off the T.V. and go to bed. She was very unhappy. Placing her hands on her hips, with anger in her voice, she spoke through gritted teeth, "If I was mean enough I could say some of the *baddest* things!"

Hair Today, Gone Tomorrow

Sometimes I refer to a bald man as being one who was about my height until he grew up through his hair.

Our daughter, Laura, was a preschooler when she noticed her PaPa Trowbridge's lack of hair on top of his head. Her description was, "PaPa's hair is incomplete on top."

Pine Floats

While visiting my older cousin Maxie one of our "projects" was to pester a teenage girl Maxie's age who worked in her father's restaurant.

Having little or no money Maxie ordered two "pine floats."

"What's a pine float?" she asked.

"A glass of water with a toothpick in it."

I Thought You Said...

At 4-H camp the leader assigned a partner or "buddy" before we went into the lake for swim time. Whenever he blew a whistle, we had ten seconds to grab hands with our buddy and hold them up. Failure to do so meant we would be "grounded" and required to get out of the water. I misunderstood him and thought he said we would be "drownded."

Another childhood misunderstanding was in Sunday School. While others sang , "I've got the peace that passeth understanding down in my heart," I thought we were singing about "a piece of plastic" understanding down in our hearts.

My wife recalls a responsive hymn that ended with the words, "and grant us Thy peace". As a child she wondered what "grantus-eye peas" were.

Won't Last Long

The opening comment of a speaker I heard a few years ago was "I know the hour is late but as Elizabeth Taylor said to her fifth husband, 'You know I won't keep you long'." (Six and seven didn't last long either.)

Divorces have been rare among the larger Beauchamp family (my grandparents, their seven children and many grandchildren, great-grandchildren and great-great-grandchildren included).

Still upset about the divorce of his grandchild, an uncle was invited to the ceremony of her second marriage. He declined. "I think I'll just wait and go to her next one."

I'll Try To Be Short . . .

The Best Or the Worst

Nothing was average with Uncle Willie. He either had the best or the worst of everything, including cars, trucks, dogs, cows, hogs, watermelons or whatever. Even the weather at his place was hottest, coldest, wettest or driest.

Lying in a hospital bed with a tubes everywhere and an IV in his arm, Daddy was visited by Uncle Willie. "How are you doing?"

Daddy explained, "Being confined to the bed with all these tubes attached makes me feel pretty miserable."

Uncle Willie quickly interjected as he jerked up his pants' leg, "Man, you don't know nothing! Just look at my shin that I scraped on the cow pen!"

Cheaper Than Most

Retail merchandising was not my calling. That impression came to me rather early in life.

A customer came in telling us that McClung (hardware) was out of one-quarter inch plywood and wanted to know if we had any. I checked our supply and found we had several sheets. He asked the price. I consulted the price list and told him it was $4.00 per sheet.

Shocked, he said, "McClung sells it for $3.75."

"Our price is only $3.50 when we don't have any."

That man must not have been too offended because he continued to purchase from our store and often asked Daddy about the young fellow who sold him the plywood.

School Days

When the start of a school year approached, Grandpa would say, "Next Monday, it will be every rat to his hole and every rat that doesn't have a hole better make one."

As a way of encouragement *and* kidding, Grandpa would ask, "Do you realize you only have a half day of school this morning?" Then he would add the disappointing reminder, "The other half will be this afternoon."

How's My What?

Some of Grandpa's vocabulary was of unknown origin. He would sometimes ask, "How's your copperosity joshuating?"

Who Do You Trust?

Many years ago Saturday was the main shopping day of the week for the farmers in our area. Stores would stay open late to accommodate shopping and visiting.

Daddy and his partner David had heard about an automobile accident near Gainesville in which the brother of Mr. Charley was injured. The phone rang at nearly 10 PM in the hardware store.

"Beauchamp Hardware," Daddy answered.

"Who is this?"

"Ottis Beauchamp. Is that you Charley?"

"Where's my wife?"

"I don't know, Charley. How's your brother? Is there anything we can do to help?"

"He's gonna make it. I want to talk to my wife."

"She's not here but I'll be glad to get a message to her."

"I called my house and I want to talk to my wife."

"Charley, I'm in the hardware store and David's here, too. You wanna talk to him?"

"Certainly not! I'd rather believe you than David."

Up In The Air

Flying in airplanes is a great time-saver. For some of us, however, it also improves our prayer life. Hymns such as "Nearer My God To Thee" come to mind when I am way up there.

Someone reminded me that Jesus said, "Lo, I am with you always."

When I fly I am very careful to not put all my weight down, sometimes keeping one or both feet off of the floor.

Wrong Word?

When our daughter, Laura, was about three years old, she had eaten a large quantity of spaghetti and much evidence of that remained on her face, hands, and clothes. Her mother prepared the bath for her and left Laura to complete the project.

After a very few minutes, Laura came into the room with a towel wrapped around her body, her face still covered with spaghetti sauce. Vera told her to get back into the tub and finish her bath.

"I can't. I already flushed it."

I wondered whether she had used the wrong word or the wrong tub.

Beauchamp Weaknesses

Grandpa Beauchamp had cataract surgery when I was a very young boy and my remembrance of him is that he always wore very thick glasses.

When I told Uncle Rufus that I would be having some minor eye surgery he told me "Beauchamps have two major weaknesses: weak eyes and weak minds."

Repeat the Good Ones

Susan was the youngest of five of us children and got a lot of attention as a child. She made some cute comment when 3 years old that brought laughter from all who heard her. She then announced, "I'm going to say *that* tomorrow".

Hello!

Before he was two years old, our grandson Joshua saw a toy telephone. The receiver, which had been connected by a string to the base, was missing. Joshua looked at it with a puzzled expression on his face and asked, "Where's the hello?"

A Dental Breakdown

A man came to my sister's house to talk to my brother-in-law. The visitor had very few teeth remaining. As he talked only two or three showed.

My toddler nephew Kyle watched the guest with great interest. He put his finger in his mouth for a little while before announcing "Daddy, I've got ten teeth. How many have you got?"

R. U. O. K.?

At the ages of 82 and 81 respectively, Daddy and Mama had each become feeble. I had pushed Daddy to the car in his wheelchair and then helped him into the front seat for a trip to the doctor. Showing her concern as always, Mama asked him, "Are you okay?"

Daddy looked at her with a sly grin on his face and replied, "Not yet. Are you?"

Truly neither was okay. The smiles they exchanged on that occasion reflected the great love story their 64 years of marriage represented.

Am I What?

Among her infirmities, Mama suffered from a significant hearing loss and Parkinson's disease.

Her neurologist checked her memory and sense of awareness during a regular office visit. After asking what year it was, pointing to a watch and asking what the object was, the doctor then asked Mama, "Who is the President?'

With a rather puzzled look she replied, "Did you say, 'Am I pregnant?'"

Backwards Again

Professor Backwards, a comic of the fifties, told about a lady running over him with her car as he was walking on the sidewalk. Belatedly she leaned her head out the car window and said, "Look out!"

His response was, "You aren't going to back up, are you?"

Uncle Rufus had driven his pickup truck through the farm gate. As he got out of the truck to lock the gate he asked his wife to pull the truck up to make room for him to close the gate. Instead she put the truck in reverse and knocked him down. She then pulled up, running over him the second time.

His injuries could have been very serious but thankfully were not. Greater injuries probably occurred to people he entertained telling that story in his inimitable style.

Oh, Say Can You See?

Daddy was an early riser. Taking two of his grandsons deer hunting one morning, they arrived before daylight near the tree stand to be used by one of the boys. Concerned that some other hunter may already be in the stand, Daddy looked up the tree and questioned, "Have you seen anything?"

If there had been anyone in the tree at that time, there was not enough light to see the ground.

Light Green

When Ovieda was in college Mama wrote a letter to her telling of some home improvement plans. Among other things she planned to paint the living room light green. My sister was concerned. She did not see any reason to paint the light in the living room at all.

Cold Feet

It was so cold one night at the hunting camp that my brother-in-law Bob said the only way he kept his feet from freezing was by tucking them up under his armpits. (I did not actually see him do that.)

A Bad Man in Archer

Before daylight, Uncle Rufus, working as a watermelon broker, left his home in Trenton traveling to South Florida. Going through Archer he realized a police car was behind him with lights flashing. Afraid there had been a family emergency, he pulled over.

The officer asked him where he was headed in such a big hurry.

"I didn't think 25 miles per hour was any indication of great haste."

"You're in a school zone and the limit is 15 m.p.h. What are you trying to do, kill some of our little children?"

"No, if I'd wanted to kill some of the children, I would have waited 'til they got out of bed."

After a stern lecture that seemed might never end, Uncle Rufus extended his hands to the officer saying, "If I'm that bad, just put the handcuffs on me and take me to jail. I'm too dangerous to be left on the streets."

"I'll not write a ticket this time but if you ever break the law again in Archer you'll be in serious trouble.

"You won't need to worry about that because I won't ever come through Archer again." He lived another 30-40 years and kept that promise.

Wind Deficiency

I read about a small boy who thought windmills were fans for cows.

A farmer who lived nearby when Daddy was a child used to have two windmills. He said he had to take one of them down because there wasn't enough wind to operate both of them.

Garden Gourmet

Fresh vegetables from local gardens, including his own, were popular food items during the seasons. Grandpa said, "I enjoy the first 200 or so messes (servings) of peas each year, but then I get kind of tired of them." After having his blood tested, he told us it was 87% pot liquor.

Easily Recognizable

Grandpa Callaway's first wife had left him and taken their young son with her leaving no information on how to contact them. For several years he wrote to other postmasters around the country searching for any clues that would help him locate them.

Finally he received a report from a postmaster in Miami indicating that his former wife was residing there. Grandpa asked a friend to drive him to Miami so he could see her in order to locate his adult son.

"After all these years you won't be able to recognize that woman," his friend said doubtfully.

"I reckon I will," Grandpa responded with confidence. "I'd know her bone on a fork handle."

Sold Out

Two young men not much older than I came into the store wanting to buy ten pounds of staples. After checking our supply, I told them I was sorry but we didn't have more than five or six pounds.

"What kind of hardware store is this, that doesn't even have ten pounds of staples?" one of them asked. "I bet McClung keeps staples in his store."

Irritated by their attitude and reference to the competitor, I struck back, "He probably does. We sell ours."

What's Her Name?

At 87 PaPa is entitled to forget some things. But he has often told a true story on himself and his faulty memory for names in the early days of his marriage nearly 60 years ago. A friend heard he had recently married and asked "Who did you marry?"

Unable to recall his bride's name, he hedged, "One of the Conerly girls."

"Which one?"

Still unable to remember Geneva, he answered, "The youngest one."

Clyde Clockweather

My move to Tallahassee from Chiefland to attend Florida State University was a classic case of country boy come to town. Actually, I was from downtown Chiefland. You could have called me naive but I wouldn't have known what that was.

The off-campus apartment enabled my roommate and me to have our own telephone for the first time. Someone had told me I could dial a certain three digit number for time and temperature. The voice said, "Time flies and money piles up when you bank at Tallahassee Federal."

I then asked, "Would you give me the time and temperature, please?"

The voice replied, "Time: 2:13 p.m. Temperature: 81 degrees."

"Thank you very much," I said as I hung up.

My roommate from Miami, Kub, laughed and explained to me that I had been talking to a machine and not to a live person. After my initial embarrassment we came up with a name for the time and temperature guy: "Clyde Clockweather". From that day on we pretended to be carrying on a conversation with our friend Clyde when we called for time and temperature.

Dr. Clyde

During exam week I developed a sty on my eye that was very uncomfortable. As I moaned and groaned about the need to study for three exams, my thoughtful roommate said, "You know what the Bible says."

"What?" I asked, not really expecting his suggestion to be very helpful.

"The Bible says, 'If thine eye offend thee, pluck it out.'"

'That's not very funny."

Shortly afterward he went to the phone and called Clyde. "Beauchamp's got a problem. He has three exams tomorrow and he can't concentrate because of a bad sty. I was wondering if you knew anything that might help him?"

Kub waited a moment as if getting a response. "That's what I told him but he's not that religious!"

He Must Be Dead

On his daily visit to the hardware store, Grandpa Callaway announced, "I'm sure sorry about old Ben!"

Uncle David questioned him, "What happened to Ben?"

"He must have died last night because he told me yesterday, 'I'll be at your house at nine o'clock in the morning if I'm living.'"

Stewed Tomaters

"What did you have for lunch at school today?" we asked our daughter, Laura, a first grader.

She named several foods followed by the horrified comment, "They had them old stewed tomaters again. And Mama, I saw one girl eatin' 'em!"

Names Are Important

While on a visit to the Memphis Botanic Gardens, Joshua, our 18-month-old grandson enjoyed feeding the goldfish, ducks and geese in the lake. As we rolled him along in the stroller a Canada goose honked loudly. Vera said, "Joshua, that goose is calling you."

Joshua turned quickly toward the goose and pointed a finger into his chest as he shouted, "Josh, Josha, Josh!" He wanted the goose to call him by name.

In Other Words

PaPa is a very special person. More than a father-in-law, he is a friend and our next door neighbor. Generally a quiet person his sense of humor is keen. He enjoys creating new words or intentionally misusing words for humorous effect.

When I first became a part of the Trowbridge family, it wasn't long before I learned that a "squanchie waunch" (or "squanch" for short) was a toilet facility... indoors or out.

A very cold day would prompt him to say, "It's cold as Floogie Coogins!" (I have never found out who she was.)

PaPa and one of his brothers entertained other tourists as they pretended to read the heiroglyphics on a large rock in the Painted Desert describing themselves as "Crockodologists".

Something that happened before daylight was "enduring the night".

Which Way?

Bud and W.O. worked together in the hardware store during their high school years. Bud was usually in a hurry to get something done so he could get off early and do the things he really wanted to do. More meditative and deliberate, W. O. moved slowly.

One project required them to deliver a truck load of wire fencing which came in large heavy rolls. The customer was an agency of the state government and the supervisor a very particular man who always wanted to do everything precisely by the book. As usual, Bud drove the truck because he got to it first not wanting W. O. to slow him down anymore than necessary.

As Bud wheeled the large truck with a dump body onto the delivery site he called out to the supervisor, "Where do you want us to dump this wire?"

The meticulous supervisor, with concern in his voice said, "Oh no! We can't have you dump it. The wire would be bent and difficult to unroll. We'll need to set the rolls off one at a time."

Obviously that was not what Bud or W. O. wanted to hear. The supervisor then pondered, "What do you fellows think? Should we stand the rolls up on end or lay them down on their sides?"

Bud's quick response oozed with sarcasm, "I'll tell you what we should do. Let's stand some of 'em up and lay some of 'em down."

Thriftmaster

Another delivery involved two pickup trucks being used to haul materials to a building site. Bud drove the newer truck while W. O. drove the older one. For entertainment purposes, I chose to ride with Bud.

On the way back to Chiefland we were ahead of W. O. but checked behind from time to time to make sure he was still following. Involved in some tale Bud was telling, we failed to look back for several minutes. When we did, W. O.'s truck was no where in sight. We turned around and went back a couple of miles to find the old truck parked on the shoulder of the road with the hood up.

Getting out at the scene of the disabled truck we asked W. O. what the problem was, as if we thought he would know or we would understand if he could tell us. The mechanical knowledge and skills of Bud, W. O. and me combined would not have been sufficient to fix a wheelbarrow.

W. O. said he didn't know what was wrong but there was a lot of smoke coming from under the hood. Looking at the engine and seeing the word "Thriftmaster" printed on the engine block, Bud announced in a voice of authority, "I can tell you what's wrong. The dang Thriftmaster is burnt up in it."

Pull Over!

"Get off the road, Uncle Rufus! Pull over!" my cousin James urged from the back seat.

"What's the matter?" Uncle Rufus asked as he continued to drive at his usual very slow speed.

"There's a fellow on Tom-walkers who wants to get by."

Lost & Found

Searching for his basketball shoes in the school locker room, Bud yelled excitedly, "I found them! Here they are with my name written on them, G-U-Y, David."

Star Of The Game

Between his fourth and fifth birthday, our son, Lance, provided much memorable material. I took him to a Florida State University football game in Tallahassee. My brother's son, Barry, sat with us and knew the names of some Seminole players. Barry would say, "Way to go Simmons!" or some other words of encouragement.

Lance began to make similar comments and a woman in front of us turned around to see where that small voice had originated. She said to Lance, "My, but you are starting out very young, aren't you?"

Looking her straight in the eye he responded, "And also, you know something else?"

She smiled and asked, "What?"

"We don't like people that smoke."

I lost all color in my face before I stammered the response, "We like the people, but not the smoke."

She didn't bother us with any more comments...or any more smoke.

Crowding Crowd

At the conclusion of that same game, I picked up my son to keep him from being trampled. A fan from a row just above us stepped down in front of us at very close range. Lance firmly told her, "Lady, you're crowding us!"

Enough Already!

On the way from the stadium that night, we were in the station wagon with my brother's family. The windows of the wagon were down as traffic moved very slowly, if at all. Some boys around ten years of age were in a car next to us and started to make conversation with my brother, who was driving the wagon.

After finding out we lived about two hours away, referring to a Tallahassee high school, one of the boys said, "I guess you know who the number one team in the state is."

From the back of the station wagon came Lance's voice, "I don't even want to hear about it!"

Show Dogs

After a large meal, consistent with Southern tradition, someone would offer Daddy more food. He often responded, "I've already eaten a pile of food a show dog couldn't jump."

How To Deal With Pain?

At nearly 80 years of age, it became necessary to have some teeth extracted.

Complaining bitterly of the pain his sore gums were causing, Grandpa removed the top of a salt shaker, poured about a teaspoon of salt into his hand, and popped it into his mouth. Momentarily, it appeared that he may pass out from the excruciating pain. When he finally caught his breath, he muttered, "Now I reckon it can hurt!"

Fisherman's Luck

After a fishing trip with a friend, the report from Grandpa was that he had not caught any, even though he had very good bait. The worm he used lasted all day. "Carter had good luck. He caught two or three like this (indicating with his fingers about two inches) and a whole bunch of little ones."

He reported his own good luck following another fishing trip. "I fell down in the boat and only broke two ribs."

Thumbs Up!

While in the home construction business many years ago, PaPa cut off the end of his thumb in a jammed table saw accident. Thumb sucking was something our son, Lance, had some reluctance to give up. In an effort to discourage that habit, PaPa told him he had sucked his so long that part of his thumb was gone. Lance told many people with great emphasis, "PaPa ate his thumb **UP!**"

Can Opener

A customer came into Beauchamp Hardware and Daddy met him with the usual, "What can we do for you?"

"I'm looking for a good can opener."

"I married one," Daddy responded .

A Young Bible Scholar

During a family summer mission project in Vermont when Lance was four, I was asking questions about the creation story. In a circle of young children I held a bean bag and asked, "Who created the heavens and the earth?"

The first child to give the correct answer, received the bean bag.

The second question stumped them all...except Lance. I asked, "What was the name of the first man God made?"

The only child to raise a hand was my son and I was so proud...until he gave the answer... "Moses."

Then I wondered why we had traveled over a thousand miles to find children who needed to learn about the Bible.

Just Like Jesus

Lance was in first grade when he came home from a church meeting of boys his age with the report, "I couldn't believe how good Dan was! He was just like Jesus... compared to Bill."

Unselfish Graffiti

Graffiti of the cleaner fifties kind was written on the dusty plate-glass windows of a vacant store building. Bud, who always enjoyed trying to aggravate W.O., wrote:
"Fools names like monkey's faces
Always seen in public places.
W.O. Beauchamp, Jr."

An Exuberant Entry

Lance was eager to start kindergarten. On the first day of school, he sprang from bed with a shout of "Yee—Hi! I'm going to school!"

The joy continued through breakfast, going to school, arriving in the classroom, seeing the other children, and getting to know his teacher. His mother was there through all of that, but when she decided it was time for her to go, school was no longer fun for Lance.

Even though he has now graduated from Stetson University, school itself has not really been much fun for him since he saw Mama leave that day.

A Brush With The Lawyer

The second day of school provided another event to remember.

Lance brushed his teeth, ran a small amount of water on the brush, and jammed it into the toothbrush holder. I slowed him down and explained that he should hold the brush under the running water and rub the bristles with his thumb to help get the toothpaste out of the brush.

"I would, Daddy, but I don't want to get all them cavities on my fingers."

Thrifty Action

As a state trooper, my brother-in-law Dick had many interesting experiences.

He stopped a speeding motorist one night and was in the process of writing a ticket. The wife of the driver stuck her head out of the passenger's window and shouted back to her husband, "James, I turned the car lights off so we can save a little bit of gas."

Get In Step!

Four semesters of R.O.T.C. were required when I attended Florida State University in the early sixties. Not interested in a military career, I was not excited about being part of the Reserve Officer Training Corps. Classroom grades were good but the two hours each Thursday were a greater challenge.

My first drill was memorable.

"If you are taller than the man in front of you, move up!"

Everyone else did.

Being slightly under five-feet, four inches, I was the shortest man in the shortest squad in the shortest platoon in the shortest company in the whole battle group.

Since we were organized by height (or lack thereof) I was usually the last man in the squad drills...until the command, "To the rear, march!" I became lead man.

During one drill I misunderstood the command. I went one way while the rest of my squad went another. I must have looked like a miniature Gomer Pyle heading west while the others were marching east.

Fall Out!

During that first drill, the platoon sergeant came over to check my nametag and shouted, "Get in step Mr. Booch-camp!" He soon learned to pronounce my name, "Bee-chum" as I do, but I never learned to march the way he or anyone else did.

Near the end of my fourth and final semester of R.O.T.C., we were preparing for "Federal Inspection" the day the regular Army officers from the Third U. S. Army came to Tallahassee to inspect our school's unit. As we practiced "pass in review" where the officers would be the next week, I felt a slap on my shoulder.

"Fall out! You've been out of step in both practices."

The day of the Federal Inspection was filled with foreboding. I didn't want to take the chance of being "outstanding in the field".

The phone rang about an hour before drill. "Beauchamp, don't come to drill today," snapped the platoon sergeant.

"Why not?"

"Report to the infirmary. Tell one of the doctors we sent you."

I did. The doctor just smiled understandingly when I told him why I was there.

Early Rising

Working in watermelon fields provided many adventures for me. Just getting to the field could be a challenge.

Uncle Willie asked me to help in his field. He wanted to get an early start the next day and suggested that he would come by for me at 5:30AM. Before five o'clock I heard his car horn blowing. A few minutes later I stumbled outside.

"I know it's going to get hot out there today so I decided we better get started early."

"Uncle Willie, if I had known you were going to come this early I wouldn't have bothered going to bed. I would've just stood in the corner and waited."

When we got to the field we had to wait for daylight so we could *find* the watermelons.

Bloodlines

Cattle ranching was the primary occupation for Uncle Rufus much of his life. He seemed to evaluate people much like assessing cattle.

When a young man got into trouble with the law, Uncle Rufus would often say, "It's the bloodline."

He would then tell about the boy's grandfather, uncle or some other family member who had gone wrong earlier.

Forbidden Fruit

Among the foods my Daddy never liked were cucumbers (unless pickled) and cantaloupes. But perhaps his most detested food was guava. He has suggested that it may have been the forbidden fruit mentioned in the Bible.

"Guava smells so bad that when my brother dropped one in the yard the family cat covered it up."

Some Do, Some Don't, Big Deal!

We brought our daughter home from the hospital when she was four days old. Five months later Laura was legally adopted. (We had been told by doctors that we would not likely be able to have children.) Two and one-half years after Laura became a part of our family, we were pleasantly surprised to learn Vera was pregnant.

As Vera began to "show" she thought it best to explain to Laura that some babies grow inside their own mothers. Other babies like Laura grow inside another person and then are adopted by people who become their Mama and Daddy.

Vera was wearing a sleeveless blouse at the time of this important discussion. A small mole could be seen under her arm, apparently attracting Laura's attention. Vera asked if Laura understood that some babies are adopted and some are not?

"Uh huh, and some people have moles under their arms and some don't."

Don't Tell Anybody

Someone said "A secret is something you tell one person at a time." Maybe it wasn't Uncle Willie who first said that but he lived it.

On many occasions Uncle Willie would come into the hardware store and call Daddy to the side with a comment like, "Ottis, come here a minute. I've got something to tell you but don't say anything about it!" When he finished that report he would speak to Daddy's partner, "Meeks, don't tell anybody but I've got something you may want to hear."

It was obvious he didn't want to be telling someone a bit of information and find out they already knew it.

Bovine Insight

Kent, my nephew, was about 7 when he was helping me throw some hay off a truck for Daddy's cows. An hour or so later I discovered that my college ring was missing. Searching the truck and the ground where the hay had been thrown, I had given up the search as a hopeless cause when Kent suggested, "Uncle Luther, you could x-ray all the cows."

Icing The Gator

On January 23, 1980, Lance's age equaled the number of digits on a normal human hand. He was, of course, a handful long before that.

The Winter Olympics of 1980 will be remembered for the U.S. upset of the Soviet Union ice hockey team for the gold medal.

My law partner at that time was a second cousin, Greg Beauchamp, who had a bachelor's degree and a law degree from the University of Florida in Gainesville. He was, and is, an avid fan of U.F. sports teams.

Lance stood at the door of my office, admiring the F.S.U. decorations and said, "Daddy, that's my best team: the Seminoles."

Then he looked in Greg's office and saw all of the Gator *junk*. "That's my next to worst team: the Gators."

Greg could not resist asking, "What's your worst team, Lance?"

"Russia!"

Known for his quick wit and sharp tongue, for one time, Greg was silent.

A Passive Child

Laura was always a very active child. We were puzzled when Lance (about six years old at the time) said at the supper table one evening, "Laura is so passive."

When we asked what he meant, Lance said, "She's always saying, 'Pass the bread, pass the salt, pass the butter'."

Make 'Em Count

Someone told me, "If you like to make the little things count, teach arithmetic to preschoolers."

A niece had received three trophies during an elementary awards program for academic achievements. One was for excellence in mathematics. On the way home, she excitedly reported to her mother, "I won two trophies last year and three this year, so I now have six of 'em."

Is that modern math or does it prove the truth of the statement I read recently? "There are only three kinds of people in the world...those who can count and those who can't."

Tasty Treats

Not much of a cook himself, Grandpa Callaway had some strong opinions about various foods. He bought peanut butter by the case and often ate it with a spoon right out of the jar.

Milk was a product he did not like at all and did not want any food that had milk as one of its ingredients. He claimed he would have been able to "taste a drop of milk in an acre pond."

Cucumbers deserved special treatment and preparation according to Grandpa. "The best way to prepare them for proper eating is to select a half dozen tender young cucumbers, soak them in ice water for two hours, then peel them carefully to make certain all of the bitter green skin is removed. Next, slice them in thin slices and place them in a glass bowl so that they look attractive. A little salt and pepper should be sprinkled on them. Add vinegar to the bowl and let them set for half an hour. Then, take them outside and throw them over the fence to the hogs!"

General Who?

While in high school I spent most Saturdays helping in the family hardware store. Saturday afternoons were rather quiet and I would be left "in charge" for awhile. One afternoon a classmate visited me in the store. Pat was a great entertainer and we had shared a lot of laughs, generally being high-school-silly.

A customer came in and from his speech and mannerisms gave the impression that he would likely shoot a good bit below par on an I. Q. course. I asked if I could help.

"Yep, I'm looking for a 'frigidairy bub'."

"A refrigerator bulb? Do you mean a light bulb that goes inside a refrigerator?"

"Yep, that's right, a frigidairy bub. You know, one of them bubs that goes up under there like this," making a twisting motion with his hand.

—————▶

Rather naive in the appliance business myself, I was uncertain whether regular light bulbs were used in refrigerators. "We have some refrigerators here. Is yours a G.E. like these?"

"That's right, General Motors," he enthusiastically responded.

As I bit my lip to keep from laughing, Pat broke the short silence with, "Fellow, what you need is a headlight!"

Unable to hold back any longer, I spat and sputtered into the face of the poor customer. I begged his forgiveness. "This guy has me in such a silly mood I can't think straight."

Fouled Out

Daron, a good friend of our children, was watching a college basketball game on television with them. After a player had committed his fifth foul, the words *"fouled out"* appeared on the screen. "Fo-**u**'-led out?" Daron questioned.

Laura was not really paying attention to the game so they asked her if she had ever had her *fo-**u**'-led* out. When she said she didn't know, they made it sound like she would be in real danger if she didn't have it out soon.

Laura is always fun for them to tease because she has a very high belief level (which is a lot nicer than saying she's gullible).

Death And Danger

A nervous bank robber told the teller, "Don't stick with me, this is a mess up!"

Grandpa Callaway said he didn't keep a gun in his house. If a burglar broke in, he would have to tell him, "Wait right here 'til I can go up to my daughter's house and borrow a gun."

He had a strong Christian faith and did not worry about death. Grandpa did say, however, "When I die, I want it to be on television because I notice that most of the actors who die in TV shows come back to life the next day."

Who's Thinking?

My brother-in-law Bob is a deep thinker. He once asked me, "What do you think about when you are not thinking?"

Further proof of the depth of his thinking came when I was in seventh grade and employed as a bag boy at a local grocery. Bob invited me to go with him on Saturday to Cross City when he went to collect rent on housing units he owned. I told him my job would make it impossible for me to go on Saturday. His response was, "Well, maybe you can go sometime when Saturday comes on Sunday."

Dependable Radar

As a state agriculture department employee, Uncle Rufus' job was to inspect hog feeding operations in his district. As he arrived in his pickup truck he spotted some dogs in the yard . "Son, will those dogs bite?" he questioned a 12 year old.

"No sir, they won't."

Exiting the truck, he walked across the yard. From under the house a small dog made a beeline for Uncle Rufus and chomped down on the calf of his leg.

"I thought you told me these dogs wouldn't bite!"

"I told you <u>those</u> dogs wouldn't bite. I *knew* 'Radar' would bite."

Selective Hearing

Johnny was a salesman for a wholesale plumbing supply company and Daddy's hardware store was one of his regular monthly stops. He was quite a talker and some of what he had to say was interesting. But he never gave anyone else an opportunity to speak.

Johnny was invited to go with Daddy to our family's farm to see the cows. My nephew Mark, a preschooler who was spending some time at the hardware store with his grandfather, went along. On the way to the farm Johnny talked constantly, hardly coming up for air. Daddy glanced down at Mark, seated in the middle, to find he had a finger stuck in each ear.

Joyful Noise

My sister Susan was singing enthusiastically, if not well, in a church group in Tampa. A friend on the row in front turned around, placed his hand on her forehead and exclaimed, "Be healed!"

It didn't work.

No Singing Aloud!

My singing ability has never been questioned. It's obvious I have none.

Our church music director sent choir members into the congregation one Sunday morning to recruit more singers for the choir. Seated near the front I was ignored as choir members approached men and women around me and further back in the sanctuary.

As they were returning to the choir loft one member asked, "Luther, has anyone invited you to join the choir?"

"No, they haven't."

Smiling he zinged me, "I'm not going to either!"

He didn't.

The End Of Smoking

One explanation I give for my height (or lack thereof) is that when I was born, Daddy passed out cigar butts. He could not have gotten them from Grandpa Callaway because he smoked them. Sometimes he would have such a short stubby cigar in his mouth he used a toothpick for a handle.

"Some people smoke their cigars as long as they can. I smoke mine as short as I can."

Acknowledgements

At least sixteen years ago, my dear wife Vera encouraged me to write a book about Grandpa Callaway. She even compiled several pages herself and presented her work to me as a "seed book" to nourish and cultivate to maturity. I didn't.

Vera has encouraged me to use my own family stories in public speaking presentations along with other humor materials. When I finally decided to write this book she became a vital part: helping me remember stories, typing, editing, arranging and encouraging. It simply could not have been done without her help.

The decision to write the book grew out of my public speaking as I realized people also wanted to hear my family stories.

Without the help of some special friends and mentors my stories would not have been heard by very many people.

The late Randy Anderson insisted that I prepare a brochure and make audio tapes of my presentations as promotional tools. His ideas helped my speaking business grow.

I spent some time in prison with "Tige" Fletcher. We were both volunteers in a Christian prison ministry. Tige recently died at the age of 90, while performing on stage for an event honoring his pastor. Tige gave me my first opportunity to entertain as a humorist outside my home area which led to other engagements. Whenever I spoke in the Orlando area, Tige was there to encourage me.

My primary mentor in the National Speakers Association is my good friend Carroll Lamb of Tallahassee. His advice and counsel have been tremendously helpful. His recommendations have opened doors for me and secured some of my best speaking opportunities.

Joe McKeever was discovered in answer to prayer. His cartoons have brought my stories to life.

A special thanks goes to Joy and John Glanzer of Glanzer Press in Newberry for their able assistance in completing this project.

Finally, my children, my brother and three sisters as well as other family members who provided the raw material for the book, are greatly appreciated.

About the Author

Luther Beauchamp is a Christian lawyer (those are not mutually exclusive terms) who lives in Chiefland, Florida, the place of his birth. He and Vera, his wife of more than thirty years, have two grown children and now enjoy the status of grandparents.

A graduate of Florida State University and the Vanderbilt University School of Law, his law practice is primarily in the areas of estate planning and administration and real estate transactions. Beauchamp is active in his church and serves as general counsel for the Florida Baptist Convention.

He is an entertaining and motivating speaker for business, church, civic and school groups, and is a member of the National Speakers Association. Demand for speaking engagements continues to increase each year throughout the Southeast.

About the Illustrator

Joe McKeever is pastor of First Baptist Church of Kenner, Louisiana as well as a cartoonist.

While obtaining a history and political science major at a Methodist college, he was called into the ministry. He then attended New Orleans Baptist Theological Seminary, earning a master of theology degree in church history and a doctor of ministry degree in evangelism.

McKeever jokes that his mom encouraged his drawing as a way to keep him occupied as a kid. His cartooning skills have enabled him to contribute to several papers across the nation, sell over 250,000 copies of his books of religious cartoons, produce an evangelistic comic book, and entertain thousands with his humor.

Order Form

Please send the following items by
Laughter's Chief Counsel,
Luther Beauchamp

_____ **Books:** I'LL TRY TO BE SHORT ...

@ $10.00 each $ _____

_____ **Audio Tapes:** @ $7.00 each

_____ LOVE IS LAUGHING MATTER $ _____

_____ SECRETARIES ARE NOT SECONDARY $ _____

_____ AMNESIA, AMBROSIA AND AMNESTY $ _____

Subtotal: $ _____

Florida residents only,
please add 7% sales tax. $ _____

Add for shipping and handling
$1.50 for the first item and
.50 for each additional item $ _____

Enclosed is a check or money order payable to:
Kidiot Productions
Post Office Box 10
Chiefland, Florida 32644

Total: $ _____

ORDERING WITH CREDIT CARD

Circle one: Please charge my   MasterCard   VISA

Account Number _____ Exp. date _____

Signature (required for credit card purchase)

SEND TO:

NAME: _____

ADDRESS: _____ Apt./Suite # _____

CITY _____ STATE: _____ ZIP _____

PHONE: (_____) _____